Build It in Public

A NOWCAST for The Kingdom.
The Days of Noah are a
signal to <u>build</u>.

DARREN THOMAS

Dedication

Great praise and honor is given to God for the impartation to write of this book. Out of millions of qualified and superior vessels, I'm always grateful God let me be on His team!

To my wife of 33+ years, Pastor Sonya, every year gets better and better. Thank you for your continued and needed push and support. There is nothing like the prayers of a partner in destiny.

To my beloved family who is my anchor and my rock: Pastor Brandon & Ciara Thomas, Preston & Crystal Thomas, Randall Thomas, along with my beautiful granddaughter, Gavyn Marie Thomas and her mother Bailey Cunningham, you know my greatest joy is the sound of "hey dad! hey pops!"

History is made crystal clear as I consider Nathan, Cortland, Cameron, Marteece, Karrington, Clyde (SonClyde and my grandson Cylen), Tyler and Tobias. God used you to make my spiritual calling so clear. While writing this book, the revelation came and I now understand I am called to be an apostolic father! Fatherhood in me is a divine call with a divine purpose.

Deacon Wallace & Cynthia Thomas are the greatest parents in the world! My siblings, Wallace Jr. (Gail) Thomas along with Pastor Terrance (Jocelyn) Thomas and my sister Min. Shniqua (Min. Julian) Walker, I have been blessed with a really great family. Mr. Jerry & Mrs. Carol Colvin, this includes you too!

To REBIRTH! You are my lifeline and my passion on earth! Thank you for the apostolic and prophetic push. Let's go higher!

To Apostle Daryl O'Neil, thank you for excellent mentorship in this transition of my life. I'm grateful for the relationship and God-connection. Thank you Bishop A. Glenn Brady for opening doors and sharing opportunities in destiny. Thank you Bishop C. Wayne Brantley for covering my greatest possession—my soul!

Thank you to everyone who plays a role in my destiny!

TABLE OF CONTENTS

BONUS:

"21 Day Decree To Change"

Build It In Public

"We have entered into the Days of Noah not merely by philosophical concept but by actual chronology. What should we do?"

Introduction

"Time must be known by revelation." To nowcast The Kingdom in strategy, position and objective, we must consider where we are in time and what we are called to do—now. Whether you are reading this book at the inception of its release or years later, the reality remains that the time signature of heaven has changed. Time is signifying to us that we are assuredly living in the Days of Noah. According to the Gregorian Calendar, Sunday, October 2, 2016 marked the commencement of Rosh Hashanah, the Hebrew or Jewish new year. According to what I refer to as the biblical calendar, at sundown on October 2, 2016 we transitioned from the year 5776 to the year 5777. This in itself is a clarion call to note and comprehend the change in heaven's time signature.

As we consider the year 5777, it reveals very important information and details that will aide us in comprehending where we are in time. In focusing on the Days of Noah, please note, Lamech (Noah's father) died when he was 777 years old. The Flood occurred 5 years after Lamech's death. It was during this period Noah was found building the Ark that was ordained by God to perpetuate life after the great Flood[1]. The sequence of the year 5777 bears the truth that we have entered into the Days of Noah not merely by philosophical concept but by actual chronology.

This chronological fact is the impetus and purpose of this book. To state what the kingdom of God must be found doing in the Days of Noah. Important to note and retain is the fact that the Days of Noah, to the world, is a clarion call to repentance and salvation before an impending doom that is prophesied in the

---

[1] The Holy Bible: Genesis chapter eight

bible. But to the church, the Days of Noah represent a clarion call to rise up and **BUILD**! In order for The Church to operate The Kingdom, it cannot find itself immobilized by fear of the end times or in possession of an escape mentality where it does no further work in the earth awaiting the second coming of Yeshua which shall carry the born-again and the dead in Christ to God before the tribulation period.

The Days of Noah to the world is a period to repent but to the church it is a period to build. In this season you are called and mandated to BUILD! Build who you are. Build what you are called to do. Build in order to fulfill your assignment. The world will be saved by what you build.

Indeed, the words of Yeshua yet resound; "many are called but few are chosen (Matthew 22:14)." In order to build, we must first shift from being CALLED to being CHOSEN. Noah's name or existence made him called. What Noah built made him chosen! If you are alive at this moment you are more than the sum result of a sexual encounter whether positive or negative. Only God can produce life. If you are alive now, it is because God has exhaled you and your purpose into this dispensation because your call is assigned to this time as a weapon in the hand of God to advance His kingdom agenda.

Noah's name means rest. This rest gave definition to his purpose or his call. However, being called does not fulfill your life's mission. Far too many individuals are immobile, resting in the glories of identifying their personal call without engaging or executing that call to its next dimension. Again, Noah's name meant he was called but what Noah built made him chosen. Noah was called to build an instrument God would use to perpetuate life and re-establish the kingdom after the Flood. In like manner, you have been given a call. It is time for you to shift from being called to the place of being God's choice. God's chosen are always identified by those who execute and actively engage in building and advancing the work of the Lord, which I refer to as the Kingdom agenda.

As you read the chapters of this book, you will be continually challenged to move to action. Execution is a missing link of today's church workers. Gathering together for worship is correct. Gathering to executive individual and corporate purpose is critical. The present day church must refrain from what I call, The Seth Syndrome. Though not the primary characters of this book, the outline of the sons of Seth versus the sons of Cain clearly portray the reason why the Kingdom must be called to action. Please note in the diagram the outline of the sons of both Seth and Cain, the remaining sons of Adam and Eve after the death of Abel.

The sons of Seth birthed a generation of descendants who became proficient in calling on the name of the Lord, or prayer, while the descendants of Cain became "builders." The Church must move from states of euphoria that allow it to cope but not excel. Many would see the sons of Seth calling on the name of the Lord as an accolade. However, while the sons of Seth were in a prayer meeting in their community, behind their four walls, the sons of Cain were taking over the world and initiating cities, buildings, technology and more without the influence of God's divine prerogative and purpose. The tragedy is, since the sons of Seth did not become builders, and thus, builders of cities, the Kingdom had **spiritual power with no earthly dominance**. The sons of Seth are forced to live in cities with cultures that were not authored by the Spirit of God. Sound familiar? God had to take an entire nation and send them into Egyptian bondage to teach them how to build cities so He could then free them from bondage so they could go and build the Kingdom. This is the importance of you grasping the criticality of this season and building what God has commanded!

As you set forth to build in this season, you must set your mental and emotional posture to comprehend. You must go into the forest alone. No one, accept God, is going with you. When God commanded Noah to build the ark, He did not send angels to serve as assistants or apprentices. Nor did God supernaturally prepare any other materials needed. He merely gave Noah the instruction and call to build and left the scene! God equipped Noah with the ability to amass and garner all the resources necessary to fulfill his call and mission. In like manner, you must expect to put in the physical, mental, and spiritual time and energy to build your assignment to its completion. Imagine how many tons of wood it took to build the ark? That meant cutting down trees and hewing wood to make it ready for use. The ark was very large, meaning a space had to be cleared to hold what Noah was planning to build before he could begin. That's a rhema word for someone reading this book right now. You have to clear a space large enough to hold the capacity of what you are building. For some, the fire of your dream is extinguished quickly because it is being suffocated by your building platform. When you get ready to build you must clear out the time, energy, resources, networks, etc. to build what you dream and that which God has assigned. When Noah completed the ark, he had to gather enough hay to make bedding for every species of animal that would reside on the ark. In addition, they would be on the ark just over a year. This means Noah had to gather various foods to sustain both his family and the animals for more than a year. According to the St. Louis Zoo, an annual grocery list for their roster of animals includes: 10 tons of carrots, 20 tons of herring, 7.5 tons of bananas, 5.5 tons of apples, 18 tons of romaine lettuce, 6 tons of primate biscuits, 85 tons of herbivore pellets, 13,000 bales of hay, 1.5 tons of squid, 15 tons of mackerel, 5 tons of smelt, 1.2 million crickets, 75 pounds of earthworms, 1.6 million mealworms, 675,000 wax worms and 22,000 adult mice and this is just a partial listing[2]. Though we are certain Noah's ark had a different food base, this listing still puts us in the mindset to comprehend producing an ark and then equipping it to function was by no means a simple task, yet God leaves it to the capable hands of Noah to bring it to completion. You too must be diligent to complete your calling and assignment and accept the intensive labor that accompanies it. It is not enough to build the assignment or the dream. You must equip the assignment and dream for perpetuation and action.

As a musician and music producer, I remember preparing for the premiere of my first oratorio FORGIVEN. It took me ten years to refine the music, vocal parts, the necessary orchestration and storyline to create the finished work. Once the oratorio was "built" I then had to "equip" it. I gathered more than 100 performers including, singers, musicians of all categories, narrators and various others to execute what I had written and scored. Once that leg was completed, I then had to gather an audience to view what we mastered in preparation and rehearsals. This included marketing, promotions, ticket sales and various other forms for advertising to motivate a city and region to gather to hear what I was called to present. I had no idea this would afford us a front-page story in the newspaper and push us to take our city's symphony hall to its capacity. This got the attention of the local symphony society who stated themselves they marveled how we took the hall to capacity. They requested that I work with them for their holiday specials to help them do

---

[2] https://www.stlzoo.org/animals/animalfoodnutritioncenter/

the same.   My performers known as MPAC or Music and Performing Arts Chorale became recurrent guests of the symphony performing with many entertainment stars and noted performers. In addition, what seemed like an insurmountable task for one individual to secure more than $25,000 budget expenses became an accomplishment because I followed the pattern of Noah in completing my dream and call. I am a witness that God will send you the assistance you need from time to time, but the majority of the work involved will come from your own work ethic.

This book is designed to use the stages of Noah's building of the ark to highlight and portray steps, tools and principles you must engage to bring God's dream into reality. Read this book to comprehend its many lessons. Refrain from reading it merely to complete it. I assure you that applying the lessons and principles included, you will be enhanced and you will be further equipped to produce what God has called you to be and do. Remember, you have been placed in this era for a specific and divine purpose.   As time continues to transition, the children are becoming the sons, the sons are becoming the fathers and the fathers are being called from labor to rest.   This is God's perpetual assignment.   Do not exit time without serving your generation. Just as Yeshua did with the Woman at The Well, God is bringing a focus to your life. Many of your life transitions have more to do with focus than punishment or despair. Remember, Yeshua points out to this woman that she had possessed five husbands and the one she possessed at that time was also not her husband. This is not merely the tale of the life or lifestyle of a woman. This woman represents the church.   The woman represents you and I.   The husbands, as the seed givers, represent that which initiates production. Yeshua is telling the woman, The Church, and you and me, we have given ourselves over to six husbands or producers who have not caused us to gender true purpose. Yeshua had to separate the woman from things that could give pleasure but not bring production. There are many of us who also suffer as this woman. We have been connected to paradigms and persons who bring momentary pleasure to our lives but still do not cause us to produce what God has said or what He is saying. Before Yeshua could get the productivity out of the woman He had to deal with her identity. In the same way, many of the experiences you have processed in recent life have to do with God bringing you to the focus you will need to become great in the Kingdom. You have a deposit to make. God and all of heaven is counting on you. Accept the challenge as Noah did and BUILD IT IN PUBLIC.

I pray this book is a main source of insight and focus for your exciting journey! May the Hand of God rest heavily upon you as you move from any and all deficiencies and set forth to be a modern-day Noah. You are The Kingdom's hope! Now therefore, arise and BUILD IT IN PUBLIC! In the Name of Rebbe, Melech HaMoshiach, the Ben Elohim Chayyim Amen.

Chapter

Build It
In Public

"It is not your

failure if they

reject what you

build, but it is

your failure

if you do not

build it because

you fear it will

be rejected."

The newspapers carry their headlines. The news anchors report their stories. The radio transmits its varied commentaries. Amid all of these and more, The Kingdom must identify its voice and give clear sight to its citizens nowcasting their position and their prophetic outcome. As Kingdom citizens, we must remember the gospel of Matthew 24:37 tells us, "For the Son of Man's coming will be just as it was in the days of Noach (CJB)." If the endtime will be as the days of Noah, judgement follows the actions of those unprepared. Salvation follows the actions of those who are prepared. That same chapter goes on to culminate in a scripture that is calling the Kingdom to action. Matthew 24:46 states, "It will go well with that servant if he is found doing his job when his master comes (CJB)." The Kingdom of God must find itself paralleling the actions of Noah. We cannot merely chart the world's judgement and impending punishment and leave the completion of our spiritual mandates and directives unfulfilled. We must do what Noah did in his time…BUILD! What you build will save you! What you build has the potential to save others.

Noah received a call from God to build something that had never been seen before. What Noah built was of such magnitude that he had to *build it in public*. He could not build a structure that large without taking the risk of being ridiculed for building it. He could not build this structure without the rush of negative emotions of fear, doubt and anxiety that would accompany it. You too have been called to build something unique to this season and time. Please comprehend the sovereignty of God determines the entrance of every soul into time. Your parents created your body, or physical being, but God exhaled your soul from Himself according to His pleasure and timing. You are alive at this time because you are called to leave your fingerprint upon this dispensation—this very moment! Begin to consider yourself as more than just a person in existence. Begin to consider yourself as more than just an individual with a purpose. *You must begin to note that you are as unique to this time as Noah was to his or Deborah was to hers.* Often times we find ourselves devaluing our contribution to the Kingdom by constantly deferring greatness to everyone else but ourselves. This book is geared to move you to the comprehension that if you do not build what God has placed in your spirit for this time, the world will go void of that gifting and the Kingdom will suffer.

You must learn how to build beyond external inspiration. Mathematical equations as simple as one plus one equals two or Einstein's energy equals mass times the speed of light squared operates the same apart from its external circumstances. Simply stated, one plus one brings the same sum whether it's raining or sunny, winter or summer, or whether an individual is motivated or not, the equation is a law and it is consistent. You must train yourself and your work ethic to be consistent no matter what the external environment may be. Please consider, God did not promise Noah perfect building conditions. Noah had to build in the cool of the day, as well as, the blazing noon day sun. He had to build whether he was highly motivated or slightly subdued. When the adversary learns that external forces can control you, he will keep you in a whirlwind because he knows that you have trained or geared yourself only to be productive in perfect conditions. What if King David did not complete his assignment after slaying Goliath because jealous Saul had a spear in his hand? What if Yeshua did not fulfill his assignment because the Pharisees and Sadducees were his enemies? We would find history resulting in defeat if these and many others did not learn how to prevail from perilous or precarious positions.

My heart is stirred when I consider one of the speeches given by notable civil rights father and leader, Dr. Martin Luther King, Jr. who stated in his speech "I Have A Dream"...

"Bull Connor next would say, "Turn the fire hoses on." And as I said to you the other night, Bull Connor didn't know history. He knew a kind of physics that somehow didn't relate to the transphysics that we knew about. And that was the fact that there was a certain kind of fire that no water could put out. And we went before the fire hoses; we had known water. If we were Baptist or some other denominations, we had been immersed. If we were Methodist, and some others, we had been sprinkled, but we knew water. That couldn't stop us.[3]"

Dr. King led a people to persevere for civil rights and voter rights in the face of grave danger, imprisonment and loss of life keeping their eyes focused as they pressed toward the mark to build in public! You and I are the same.

Remember the biblical account of Sanballat, Tobiah, and Geshem in the book of Nehemiah 4. They jeered the Israelites for rebuilding the wall of Jerusalem. Israel had to learn to keep building even in the face of public accusation. Also, in the Gospel of John 9, Yeshua teaches us a valuable principle that sometimes it will not be those in the world who lack the comprehension of your call. Sometimes it may even be carnal, superficial, or shallow believers who herald blanket statements and accusations to appear to have knowledge though their words are shrouded with blatant ignorance. Consider this passage as we recall John 9:1-3 which states,

---

[3] http://www.americanrhetoric.com/speeches/mlkivebeentothemountaintop.htm

"1 As He passed by, He saw a man blind from birth. 2 And His disciples asked Him, "Rabbi, who sinned, this man or his parents, that he would be born blind?" 3 Jesus answered, "It was neither that this man sinned, nor his parents; but it was so that the works of God might be displayed in him.""

This passage teaches us that often "what people cannot define— they curse." The disciples were carrying a pseudo depth of perception for any number of reasons including being the elite who walked with Yeshua or having been the first to be established as His disciples. Whatever the reason, they did not know what God was doing so what they could not define as the move of God they immediately equated it with a work of the devil. Yeshua had to explain the reason the man was born blind had nothing to do with sin. The man was born blind so God's works could be displayed in him at a particular time in life. Yeshua displayed the example of how to build a miracle even when the public opinion within the church does not understand and cannot discern what you are doing. Find yourself beyond the trap of public opinion and keep building. The word of God on your life must be the single most motivating force. Sometimes those in mainstream society, or even those in your circle, will not understand who you are and regretfully sometimes those in the church will not understand either.

"what people cannot define —they curse"

I remember a lesson from psychology called The Johari Window[4] which is used to assist individuals in comprehending their relationship with themselves and others. The Johari Window

---

[4] https://www.psychologytoday.com/blog/sideways-view/201511/self-awareness

uses a single window with four window panes: 1) Open Self, 2) Blind Self, 3) Hidden Self and 4) Unknown Self.

Open Self	Hidden Self
Blind Self	Unknown Self

Johari's Window

Open Self is defined as information about you that both you and others know. Blind Self is defined as information about you that others know but you do not know. Hidden Self is defined as information about you that you know but others do not know. Unknown Self is defined as information that neither you or others know.

I favor this illustration because it brings to light that there is a portion of your life and call that you and others will know. There is a portion of your life and call that you know about yourself but others do not know. There is another portion of your life and call that others know but you do not know. And finally, there is a portion of your call that neither you or others know. So what do you do? Find yourself mastering the last two window panes. This is the part of your life and destiny that is given over to a unique and select group of others who are assigned to your destiny. These include parents who are normally the first individuals responsible for cultivating who you are in God. Others will include pastors who provide spiritual insight and counsel. Prophetic individuals who see the hand of the Lord upon you and can identify or nowcast where God is and what you must do. And finally, Apostles who are assigned to activate your gift, often multiple times, as your gifting or calling is promoted or revealed over time.

You are very unique to the time in which you live. The tug or push you feel in your spirit is God calling you to a needed task that will alter history and most importantly build The Kingdom. Do as John declares in Revelation 3:11, "...hold fast what you have, so that no one will take your crown."

BUILDING FOR TRANSITION

When God called Noah to build the ark, there were several layers of purpose involved. For our emphasis today, I call to your attention this fact: **"If you do not build it, you will remain in yesterday's curse rather than tomorrow's promise."**

When God told Noah to build the ark, Noah was not only building for obedience, he was building for transition. What Noah built is going to carry him out of the curse of the Flood into the promise of a new day. How many times have we cried out to the Lord for blessings, miracles and breakthroughs with the blueprints for the ark in our hands without a manifestation of the same? The blueprints or the idea of the ark did not save Noah. The building of the blueprints or idea did! When God establishes a means of blessing, no prayer line, altar experience or faith seed is going to counteract nor replace God's command and plan. The way out is to build what God said. Many individuals find themselves delaying their deliverance by building counterfeit purposes in an attempt to bypass the process of authenticity. In Noah's scenario, worship alone would not have been a replacement for the ark. Prayer alone would not have been a

Many individuals find themselves delaying their deliverance by building counterfeit purposes in an attempt to bypass the process of authenticity.

replacement for the ark. Even a healing ministry would not have been a replacement for the ark. When God calls you to a specific task, there is no replacement for the completion of that task. God could be calling you to write a book but you choose to sing in the choir, join the ushering team or altar workers. Though all of these are valuable positions, none of them are a replacement for building what God said to do in the moment.

A biblical example of this principle is found in the story of Abraham and Sarah. God promised Abraham and Sarah a son who was to be the heir of God's promise made to Abraham. When Sarah considered the time of life, she suggested that Abraham have relations with one of the servant women in the house whose name was Hagar. Abraham acquiesced and went into Hagar and produced Ishmael who was not the seed promised to Abraham by God. Both Abraham and Sarah had to learn that Sarah's womb was not barren, it was on assignment to produce Isaac according to God's timing and not their age or physical circumstances. They built a counterfeit son in an attempt to bypass the process of authenticity which glorified God showing that He was able to keep his word even beyond the parameters of natural definition.

You and I must learn to accept the challenge of authenticity which is often of great price. Being an individual who loves fashion, I have a certain category of items that I purchase that I choose from particular designers. These items often cost three to four times the amount I could pay for the knockoff or look alike. Others sometimes try to persuade me to settle for the imitation because it is cheaper. However, I prefer to save money over time in order to buy what is real rather than what is fake. I have learned that the real thing lasts years longer than the subpar imitation that show various signs of being a lower quality.

I challenge you as I challenge myself to start or continue to master the process of authenticity so when you build your ark it can stand the tests of time, outside forces and spiritual attacks and engender that which God desires. When Noah built the ark he was also building a transition to promise. You too will experience another level of success when you take on the weight of completing the task to which you are called. The dream of God for you is not only for others, it is for you as well. The book you are assigned to build will bless others but bring you blessing. The business you are called to build will service others but afford you wealth. If you do not build the ark/the call you will be found with others, drowning in the curse rather than moving forward to the blessing.

IT DESTROYS AND IT DELIVERS

When God sent the rain to earth and opened the fountains of the deep, what killed others saved Noah. What destroyed the earth was the transport that carried the ark to promise. Remember, when thick and dense darkness was widespread throughout Egypt there was light in Goshen for the Hebrews. Yes, the cross was the platform upon which Yeshua gave his life, but is was also the platform from which He ascended to heaven to be found accepted in His sacrificial purpose. When you complete the dream of God, a season that may be creating unemployment for others, will generate a sustaining force for you!

According to Investopedia, Warren Buffet, John Paulson, Jamie Dimon, Ben Bernanke and Carl Icahn were among the savvy investors who knew how to acquire wealth even during challenging times including the great credit crisis of 2008. They knew how to master statistics and forecast the future to make viable choices that caused them to excel when others went broke. You and I must be the same way in the Spirit. The newspapers and news reports are filled with bad news. Our day is filled with crime stories at a rate that could make you desire to lock yourself in a compound and never come out. Many in places of power offer forecasts for the future that are bleak. However, we must know how to position ourselves according to the scriptures. The Gospel of Luke guides us through the thoughts of Yeshua as it states in Chapter 21,

> "25 There will be signs in sun and moon and stars, and on the earth dismay among nations, in perplexity at the roaring of the sea and the waves, 26 men fainting from fear and the expectation of the things which are coming upon the world; for the powers of the heavens will be shaken. 27 Then they will see the Son of Man coming in a cloud with power and great glory. 28 But when these things begin to take place, straighten up and lift up your heads, because your redemption is drawing near."

Yeshua is telling us of one account with two different time signatures. Yes, in the end time there will be dismay and distress. Yes, at the close of time there will be perplexities and men who will faint or give up as the result of fear. However, we must note, these signs tell us what will happen in the "world." Yeshua goes further to state in verse 28 the sign belongs to The Kingdom. He declares when the negative signs are occurring in the world The Kingdom must straighten up and lift up our heads for our redemption is drawing near. Far too often I hear many individuals declare the world's signs to the church and leave the church with no signs of their own. What this passage tells us is there is one time with two different signs that give information on how to interpret the time.

This is what must be understood about Noah's building of the ark. The same flood that would destroy the earth would provide the waters that would deliver the ark to its new destination. You must comprehend that though the time or circumstances in which you are living may be rough, always rehearse that **time must be known by revelation** and the revelation you may receive is that your rough moment is always your launching moment!

You are assigned by God. Heaven is at your disposal. The Kingdom of God is your headquarters. The Church is your launch pad. Build your assignment and keep building until it is complete. We need you and we're depending upon you to win! There is no more time to hide or to retreat to fear. God has more who are for you than you will ever have against you. Exit this chapter with one command—BUILD!

Those
You
Carry

Chapter

"Every promise and blessing of God much shift to its third dimension."

On Noah's ark were eight individuals: Noah, his wife, his three sons, and their wives. From this detail are several examples that exhibit the consistency of God's word. Proverbs 13:22 tells us, "A good man leaves an inheritance to his children's children, And the wealth of the sinner is stored up for the righteous." This means a good man leaves an inheritance for his generation, the generation after him, and the generation after. This principle is clearly found in those who were aboard the ark. Noah and his wife represent the present generation. His sons represent the next generation, and his son's wives represent the children unborn to time or the generation after that. God set up three generations to propel life and the advancement of The Kingdom in the new world. This is a valuable lesson. Because what you build carries you to your new world or your promised opportunity, you are not just building for yourself. You are building for your generation and the two generations after you.

Three Dimensions Aboard The Ark

Every promise and blessing of God must advance to its third dimension to be fully manifested or fully experienced. There are three levels or dimensions to a blessing or promise. Level one is the promise established. Level two is the promise manifested. Level three is the promise distributed. A blessing or promise must move to the distribution stage to maximize its full potential. Many individuals in the Kingdom house frustration because they spend the majority of their years in level one. Others have received a word of prophecy or instruction at a revival, conference, convention or other service. And while this is important, it is not the only step to receiving the promise, it is just the beginning. The power of that promise will be in the third dimension or the distribution level. It is awesome to have God make a promise to you, however, you must note that a promise made is not a promise manifested. **Every prophecy from God must have a strategy in order for it to be fulfilled**. A prophecy without a strategy is frustration and a missed opportunity waiting to happen. Until that promise is processed it is something to hope for, but not something to be realized. Yeshua was and is God's prophetic plan of redemption. Revelation 13:8 proclaims that The Lamb—Yeshua—God's Plan of Redemption was slain before the world was founded. However, the prophecy had a strategy. A child would be born of a virgin, die upon a cross, and be resurrected from the grave affording redemption to those who call upon His Name. The Son of God was a prophecy in eternity before He became The Lamb slain in the realm of time. God's prophecy had a plan and we are saved by its fulfillment.

Consider Abraham as the promise of God *established*. God told Abraham in Genesis 17:19, "No, but Sarah your wife will bear you a son, and you shall call his name Isaac; and I will establish My covenant with him for an everlasting covenant for his descendants after him." This is the promise of God established. In Genesis 21:2-3 we recall,

> "2 So Sarah conceived and bore a son to Abraham in his old age, at the appointed time of which God had spoken to him. 3 Abraham called the name of his son who was born to him, whom Sarah bore to him, Isaac."

Isaac being born represents the promise of God *manifested*. A final account is found in Genesis 25:26 and in Genesis 35:22-26. The first passage reads, "Afterward his brother came forth with his hand holding onto Esau's heel, so his name was called Jacob; and Isaac was sixty years old when she gave birth to them." Here we have Jacob being born to Isaac. The last passage reads,

> "22...Now there were twelve sons of Jacob— 23 the sons of Leah: Reuben, Jacob's firstborn, then Simeon and Levi and Judah and Issachar and Zebulun; 24 the sons of Rachel: Joseph and Benjamin; 25 and the sons of Bilhah, Rachel's maid: Dan and Naphtali; 26 and the sons of Zilpah, Leah's maid: Gad and Asher."

In summation, the promise of God was *established* in Abraham, *manifested* in Isaac and *distributed* through Jacob. It was not until the promise moved to its third dimension that the Twelve Tribes or the Nation of Israel was born. In like manner, you too must shift your promise to its third dimension. Remember, as you build, you are not just building for yourself. You are building for the next two generations. This is the power of distribution.

There are many examples of this pattern in the scriptures, however, we will look at one additional example. We comprehend that God is Almighty. This is God establishing the knowledge of who He is to mankind. According to 1 John 3:8, "For this purpose the Son of God was manifested, that he might destroy the works of the devil." The Son is manifested to bring salvation to the world and to destroy the works of the devil. This is the power of God manifested. In the final dimension, the power of God is distributed in the Holy Ghost. John 14:16-17 says,

> "16 I will ask the Father, and He will give you another Helper, that He may be with you forever; 17 that is the Spirit of truth, whom the world cannot receive, because it does not see Him

30

or know Him, but you know Him because He abides with you and will be in you."

Thus Acts 1:8 states, "but you will receive power when the Holy Spirit has come upon you..." The Holy Ghost distributed in mankind gives all people the power to engage heaven on earth and to further advance the mission of The Kingdom. This is another example of the power of the third dimension or shifting to the spiritual stage of distribution.

The more you understand about those you carry, whether they are family members, business partners, a congregation or members of a group in general, the more you will comprehend their purpose and your role in their destiny.

THE DEFINITION OF RELATIONSHIPS

Remember, there are eight people aboard the ark: Noah, Noah's wife, Noah's sons and Noah's son's wives. This not only tells us about people and their roles, it explains and gives an example of the level of productivity needed to fully engage what God has given you. To bring the full level of productivity to manifestation, Noah must engage two dimensions of productivity. The men on the ark represent things or individuals that beget and the women represent things or individuals that produce. Do not become entrapped in thinking of a hierarchy or gender roles. These are merely sighting two types of people aboard the ark. What the scripture illuminates is a higher definition of purpose. Those present on your ark (dream, vision, idea, etc.), which can be classified as your network, must have the ability to beget and produce. Individuals in your network who do not show the fruits of being able to beget or produce are normally individuals who possess an opinion without and obligation. When a person in your network merely has an opinion without an obligation, that person will often become a hindrance or a point of frustration. Opinionated people have something to say about everything while feeling obligated to do nothing about anything.

When a person in your network merely has an opinion without an obligation, that person will often become a hindrance or a point of frustration.

You must come to realize and note: **"do not carry them if they do not see what you see."** Noah's family had to trust in what Noah told them God said; which took a level of faith, trust, and personal vision to believe that something that they had never seen before—an ark—was going to save them from something they had never experienced before—a flood. In like manner, there will be ideas you possess that your network must understand, while others in the general population will not understand. Your network must see what you see and comprehend their role in its fulfillment.

This is why Apostle Paul tells us in Hebrews 12:1, "Therefore, since we have so great a cloud of witnesses surrounding us, let us also lay aside every encumbrance and the sin which so easily entangles us, and let us run with endurance the race that is set before us." The cloud was Israel's network. The cloud was the testimony and faith of individuals who guided them as they pursued their place in promise and the fulfillment of God's will. The cloud was comprised of those who are listed in Hebrews Chapter 11 as being the faithful. Let us consider the meaning of their names:

ABEL	BREATH
ENOCH	INITIATES
NOAH	REST
ABRAHAM	NATION OF MULTITUDES
ISAAC	WILL LAUGH
JACOB	HELD BY THE HEEL; TRICKED
JOSEPH	GOD WILL ADD
MOSES	TAKE OUT; DRAW OUT
RAHAB	IN SECRET
GIDEON	CUT DOWN
BARAK	LIKE LIGHTNING
SAMSON	LIKE THE SUN
JEPHTHAH	GOD SETS FREE
DAVID	BELOVED
SAMUEL	GOD HAS HEARD

When the meaning of each name is put in sentence form it states: **"The Breath of God initiates rest to a nation of multitudes who will laugh. Though they were tricked, God will add and take out in secret and will cut down, like lightning, (those who tricked the multitudes). Then, like the sun, God sets free His beloved because He has heard them."**

This is the power of knowing those you carry and ensuring you have the right people with you. Those aboard your vessel, your dream, or your strategy should be those assigned to assist you in fulfilling your God-given commission. First Thessalonians 5:12 says, "And we beseech you, brethren, to know them which labour among you, and are over you in the Lord, and admonish you;" You must know the expertise and giftings of those who are laboring among you. Aaron Rodgers of the Green Bay Packers stated, "Surround yourself with really good people. I think that's an important thing. Because the people who surround you are a reflection of you." Take a look at those in your network or those who are close friends and then ask yourself "what do I look like?"

THE SUPPORT STAFF

Have you ever asked yourself why did God create animals? Animals were the support system given to Adam to secure and perpetuate the ecosystem of the earth. Without animals the ecosystem and thus the earth itself would be thrown out of balance. Without the animals, the creation would be out of synch. Have you ever correlated the fact that Adam could not have dominion in the earth nor could he dress and keep the garden without this support staff. Noah, a type of Adam, could not forge the new world and reestablish it without this same support system—animals. Paralleling the animal kingdom to your destiny, you too must have a support system on board that can aid you in establishing your vision or mission. Certainly, we are not referring to people as animals, however, we are layering and paralleling revelation and study to comprehend what God is saying.

Genesis 2:19-20 says,

"19 Out of the ground the Lord God formed every beast of the field and every bird of the sky, and brought them to the man to see what he would call them; and whatever the man called a living creature, that was its name. 20 The man gave names to all the cattle, and to the birds of the sky, and to every beast of the field..."

Immediately after God put Adam in the garden to cultivate it, the support staff (animals) are brought to Adam for him to designate, task, and set in place. The cultivation of the garden and subsequently the earth is impossible without them. As a matter of fact the support staff is so important that God generates their presence before He sets Adam to performance. Before Adam can cultivate he must CALL. Adam must call the animals by their ability and character and set them in place. The support staff is unseen in importance by the multitudes (except by those who seek an understanding or who are builders themselves) but are vital to the success of the mission.

As a music producer, I write, orchestrate, and present oratorio performances. Before we reach the premiere at the symphony hall, months earlier and sometime years, I put together a support team that is vital to my success. Those individuals comprehend my vision and commit themselves to its completion. They are the unseen, but present force that gives movement to the vision. The unseen, but present force, secures the venue, books the hotel rooms, prepares the performance manuals, schedules the caterer for the rehearsal dinner, and so many other vital tasks that are unseen in the performance but vital to its success. This is what the animals provided for Adam. They were the unseen, but present force, that allowed the performance of cultivating the garden to even be possible.

Even in the ecosystem of today, the average individual does not think of the importance of bees, certain moths and other insects that pollinate plants that ultimately provide food or other necessary components. We do not consider the fish that eat algae or even the excrements of other fish to maintain life in the ocean. We may not even know of the oxpecker bird which feeds from the ticks that live on giraffes, as well as eating diseased wound tissue from particular animals that allows the wound to heal free from disease or infection[5]. What if planarians, other flatworms, certain crabs, and shrimp did not eat fish detritus and other sea creature waste[6]? We may see it as insignificant. Others may not even know it occurs, but these and many other vital processes keep the earth cultivated and perpetuated.

GOD CREATES THEM, YOU CALL THEM

Genesis 2:19 "Out of the ground the Lord God formed every beast of the field and every bird of the sky, and brought them to the man to see what he would call them; and whatever the man called a living creature, that was its name." In your pursuit of success, do not attempt to cultivate your garden alone. God has already created a support system that is designed for you to assist you in fulfilling your dream. Hear me — "When God gives a directive, the support system is included." God gave Adam the command to cultivate the garden, then formed every creature necessary to bring it to pass and brought them to Adam. All Adam had to do was name and activate his support staff. With this in mind, please note: **"Who calls you—is not always who God called."** When you have a God-given support, it is effortless, often for a lifetime, and fluid in the completion of your dream or mission.

The completion of the oratorios I previously mentioned, had a support staff that was priceless. A support staff often fills in and completes tasks that you are not equipped to fulfill. Even the President of the United States operates by the wisdom and input

---

[5] http://animals.mom.me/relationship-between-oxpecker-bison-3153.html

[6] http://www.fishforums.net/threads/what-eats-fish-waste.156759/

of a cabinet of leaders who possess given areas of expertise that equip him or her to make crucial decisions. For me, I have never done an oratorio without Regina Lisbon as Vocal Director, Dr. Alton Merrell, Jr. as Music Director, G. LeRon Rainey as Music Coordinator, and my wife, Pastor Sonya, as Intercessor. Certainly, and to be fair the list is far more extensive, but I noted these to show the importance of the support team. These individuals compensate in the areas where I am deficient or may go lacking because my time and skill must be placed in other areas. I admonish you to find your support team and caution you not to name them by your friend pool. Instead, name your support team by those whom God has called and chosen and you will never regret it. They make a valuable difference in the fulfillment of God's will for your life.

GO FOR YOUR KIND

God's order in Creation gives us a final lesson to consider. Genesis 1:24 reads, "And God said, Let the earth bring forth the living creature after his kind, cattle, and creeping thing, and beast of the earth after his kind: and it was so (KJV)." There is power in comprehending the knowledge of who you are and being surrounded by those of like kind. Creation was accomplished by having the universe, the animal kingdom, nature, and people in order. Seed bearing fruit was in a group. Animals emerged by their grouping. Even the fish of the sea came into being according to their designation. Man was made according to his classification which was and is in God's image. As the previous list illustrated, you must be found with those who are "after your kind." You need individuals in your network who see what you see, as well as, those who comprehend who you are and can help mold you and shape your destiny. Avoid fitting in groups,

> ## "If you merely become the opinion of others, you will become a misfit to the opinion of God."

associations, or even small groups of friends of individuals who do not or cannot comprehend your purpose. If you merely become the opinion of others, you will become a misfit to the opinion of God.

Those you carry are called by God to assist you in destiny. Study them. Know them. Afford them power to assist you. You are on your way to a great place in God. He has you reading this book on your journey to guarantee it!

The Raven And The Dove

Chapter

"God will assign people to your transport who are not assigned to your purpose."

When the waters of The Flood began to recede, Noah found himself on Mount Ararat. This is significant as we will note in Chapter 4, Ararat means the curse is reversed. However, there is another significance paralleled to God's principle and purpose. Noah's Ark rested on the top of Mount Ararat because God's position for The Kingdom has always been a mountain since the Garden of Eden. We know Eden was on a mountain because we are told in Genesis Chapter 2 of a river that issued from the garden and then became four rivers. Geographically rivers find their origin on a mountain. The mountain represents the place of power and might. A mountain is representative of a system— Godly or ungodly. So just as with the Adamic model, God set Noah (a type of Adam) on a mountain to perpetuate the new world after The Flood because God's establishment of The Kingdom is atop a mountain.

As the waters began to recede further, there are two occurrences that demand our consideration to elucidate a strategy and purpose. Genesis 8:6-12 reads,

> 6 Then it came about at the end of forty days, that Noah opened the window of the ark which he had made;
> 7 and he sent out a raven, and it flew here and there until the water was dried up from the earth.
> 8 Then he sent out a dove from him, to see if the water was abated from the face of the land;
> 9 but the dove found no resting place for the sole of her foot, so she returned to him into the ark, for the water was on the surface of all the earth. Then he put out his hand and took her, and brought her into the ark to himself.

10 So he waited yet another seven days; and again he sent out the dove from the ark.
11 The dove came to him toward evening, and behold, in her beak was a freshly picked olive leaf. So Noah knew that the water was abated from the earth.
12 Then he waited yet another seven days, and sent out the dove; but she did not return to him again.

Here we see the raven was released first and only once. The Raven did not return to Noah. The dove was released three times and returned twice. The dove did return to Noah. There are several lessons to be learned from this detail, however, for this book we shall only deal with those associated with the established theme.

THE RAVEN AND THE DOVE

The raven and the dove represent two types of individuals that are a part of your transport to your new tomorrow, your promise — your destiny. These two sectors of people are required as a part of your transport. You must learn how to master them to your advantage.

First, the bible says the raven circled the ark and flew to and fro. A picture will become clearer as we establish what the bible is saying and add that definition to our thinking. The Hebrew word for "to and fro" is YATSA[7] meaning "to" and SHUMB[8] meaning "fro." When the bible says the raven went to

---

[7] https://www.blueletterbible.org/lang/lexicon/lexicon.cfm?Strongs=H3318&t=KJV

[8] https://www.blueletterbible.org/lang/lexicon/lexicon.cfm?Strongs=H7725&t=KJV

and fro until the waters of the flood were abated, it is not giving a picture of the raven wandering aimlessly above the water never resting, but continually flying. The bible is telling us the raven flew out into the sky and returned back to the ark until the waters were dried from the earth. After the raven was released from the ark it never returned to Noah, but it did return to the ark. The words YATSA and SHUMB are explaining the raven flew to and fro from the ark (as its landing station) but never to Noah.

The raven is called to be on the ark just like the dove, but with another purpose and another mission. Notice the raven is released from the ark while the dove is released from Noah. **The raven represents people who are assigned to your transport, but not your destination of purpose.** Noah is assigned to bring the raven to the new world just like he is assigned to bring the dove. However, once the ark fulfills its transport or its purpose, the relationship between it and Noah is complete.

Every person in your network or on your team is not necessarily a member for life. Some relationships are transitional relationships and are not for the duration of your ministry or business. Certainly, there are opportunists who will seek to utilize what you have for their selfish purposes. Howbeit, there will be several times in your ministry and career where you will be assigned to get a person or a group from point A to point B and that's it. Noah is the transport, but not the destination. Remember, the earth is completely covered by water so the raven could not have flown, for 14 days straight, waiting for trees or certain tall shrubs to appear. The raven used the ark as a landing and launching place of its own volition and outside of any connection to Noah. In plain terms, the raven utilized the ark to get from the old world to the new world and that was all. When

Noah released the raven, his assignment was fulfilled. The raven was under Noah's watch, but only for a particular period.

Remember, Judas was assigned to Yeshua and the Garden of Gethsemane but not to Calvary. Certainly, at a point Yeshua knew this. However, He did not seek to harm or oust Judas though He knew Judas' intent. Temporary people make their own segue out of your life. When they do—let them. Do not lament their exit. Do not attempt to attach their exit to your success or failure. When a person or group makes their exit, you must remain focused on your assignment. Their exit does not detract from your purpose or your goals. God has someone in your network, like He had on the ark, who will step in and fulfill the need with your heart in mind. Know how to master temporary individuals as much as you know how to master or unitize the skills of the long-term relationship.

Next, as we consider the dove, let us quickly recall the scripture tells us Noah sent out the dove three different times to survey the land. Again, when we carefully consider text and proper definitions we will learn much about the scene as it unfolds. Genesis 8:8 reveals, "Then he sent out a dove from him, to see if the water was abated from the face of the land..." First, please note the difference in the launch of each bird. The raven was merely sent out. The dove was sent from Noah—himself. As the bible carefully depicts the account, Noah sending forth the dove from himself is defining that Noah sent the dove from his NEPHESH or soul. The raven has a connection to the ARK, but the dove has a connection to NOAH. The dove being released from Noah's soul reveals, unlike the raven, the dove is connected to Noah and his purpose. The dove is assigned to the fulfillment of Noah's call. This immediately highlights the point that there are those connected to your purpose or your call that are assigned by

God to assist you in fulfilling the same. Just as the dove went out and surveyed the land and returned to Noah, God has assigned someone to you and you to someone to assist in the fulfillment of His purpose. Again, do not be distracted or dismayed by temporary relationships in destiny. God has a person or persons assigned to you that will gather resources for your destiny and return to you with the report or that which is needed.

THE MISSION OF THE DOVE

The parallel between the old testament ark—Noah's Ark and the new testament ark—Yeshua, will reveal to us the work and this mission of the Holy Spirit in operation in your life. Genesis Chapter 8 gives us the knowledge that Noah sent out the dove (from himself) three particular times. Let us look at a comparison to gain an understanding of what God wants you to expect in this season.

NOAH ARK - Old Testament Ark	YESHUA - New Testament Ark
The First Presence of The Dove	The First Presence of The Dove/ Holy Spirit
• The Dove returns to Noah (himself) - Genesis 8:9 • This signified to Noah that salvation to the new land was established though not yet manifested—time to exit the ark.	• The Holy Ghost Overshadows Mary and enters her womb - Luke 1:35 • This is the salvation of God established though unborn or not yet manifested.
The Second Presence of The Dove	The Second Presence of The Dove/Holy Spirit
• The Dove returned to Noah with an olive leaf - Genesis 8:11 • This signified that the promise is manifest but not ready for habitation.	• The Dove descended on Yeshua like a dove. - Luke 3:22 • This signified that The Promise is manifest, however it is not yet time for human habitation.

NOAH ARK - Old Testament Ark	YESHUA - New Testament Ark
The Third Presence of The Dove	The Third Presence of The Dove/ Holy Spirit
• The Dove is sent out but does not return - Genesis 8:12. • This signified that all things are made ready for life to begin and be perpetuated in the new world.	• Yeshua yielded up The Dove/ The Ghost and The Dove/Holy Spirit never returned to the body of His flesh. - Matthew 27:50 • This signified that all things were ready for Pentecost where the Spirit would not inhabit men in the new world called The Kingdom.

Just as there was a three dimensional shift of the dove for Noah, and a three dimensional shift of The Spirit in Yeshua, there is a three dimensional shift of The Spirit of God in you! The first shift was when you received the Holy Spirit as indicated in The Book of The Acts of The Holy Spirit Chapter 2. The second shift is the Spirit of God resident in you giving you the power to "be" as indicated in Acts 1:8. The third shift is the flow of the gifts of the Spirit in ministry as indicated in 1 Corinthians Chapter 12. You are God's last ark in the earth! Noah's ark came through water, then was descended upon by a dove. Yeshua came through the water in baptism and the Spirit descended upon Him as a dove. When you were baptized, you too, came through the water like Noah's Ark and Yeshua in Jordan. Then, just as with Noah's Ark and Yeshua, the Spirit of the Lord descended upon you! You are ready to build the new world called The Church— The Kingdom of God on earth.

Who you are is vital to this time. You must comprehend the unfolding of this chapter and master those under your charge of ministry scope. You are assigned to transport some to the new world, while others are assigned to you to assist you in fulfilling your call. Maximize your call! You have come through the waters of life, tragedy, challenge, and time. You have been delivered to this very important signature in time to transport as many as possible into the new world (The Church/The Kingdom) before the rapture. All arks in place! Build It In Public! There is a world to save; a revival to stir!

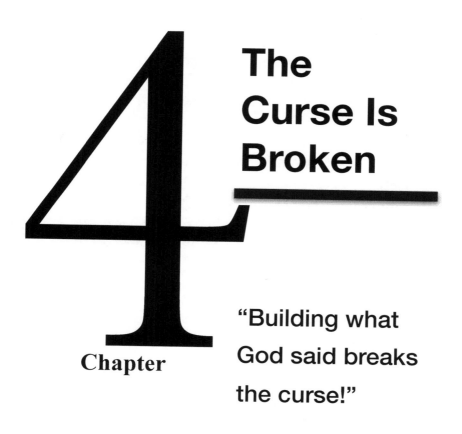

The Curse Is Broken

Chapter

"Building what God said breaks the curse!"

There were dimensional benefits attached to Noah's accomplishment of God's directive in the building of the ark. One of the things that precipitated God's command for the ark to be built is found in Genesis 6:5, "Then the Lord saw that the wickedness of man was great on the earth, and that every intent of the thoughts of his heart was only evil continually." Man's power to bring into being was tainted and manipulated so severely that every one of his thoughts and intents were perpetually evil. In the midst of this God commands Noah to build an ark. Noah's purpose in life was the meaning of his name. Noah, which means rest, was born to bring rest to earth, his family, and God's purpose for man to establish the Kingdom of Heaven on earth. In the consistency of God's pattern, Noah's typology is Adamic. He is sent by God to establish the earth, perpetuate God's purpose of population, dominion, replenishing and subduing the earth.

At the conclusion of The Flood of Noah, the ark rested at the top of a mountain called Ararat. Strong's Concordance of The Bible tells us according to reference H780 Ararat means "the curse is reversed." The ark left from a place of perpetual evil and landed on a place called the curse is reversed! But before we deal with the reversing of the curse, we must consider the message that is hidden in the location of where the ark rested.

We have just noted the ark landed on Mount Ararat. But there is more to pull from that location. Interestingly enough, Ararat is "east" in Armenia or Land of Aram in Hebrew and is watered by four rivers. This is the Edenic model! I remember hearing one of the profound messages of Honorable Bishop Tudor Bismark who taught me "once God establishes a pattern, He seldom deviates from it." Just as God set Adam in Eden, geographically, Ararat and the land surrounding it is set forth in the same pattern for Noah to re-establish the post flood earth just as Adam did.

Ararat was also situated between a river and two lakes. The River Araxes, and the lakes, Van and Oroomiah[9]. Being a student of biblical typology, I was immediately intrigued by the fact that Noah's ark came to rest between three bodies of water because of the fact that water is a type for Spirit. In further study, I found the River Araxes is from a Hebrew word which means "the city of the Remnant[10]." As I study the Hebraic Roots of Christianity course work at the university I attend, I have come to realize that a remnant is not something left over or a residual. Rather, a remnant is a capacity to reestablish. This is remarkable that the curse is reversed in a place that has the capacity to reestablish.

Remarkably the geographic cues given to us by the information surrounding Mount Ararat teaches us many things. When you build what God has called and commanded you to build, you will find yourself in a spiritually empowered place. You are building to leave the place of the curse and arrive at your personal Eden where you must then establish the Kingdom of Heaven on earth. This is an apostolic call and an apostolic mission. Building what God has commanded gives your life a divine RESET that carries you to original purpose and original productivity. When you build what God has directed, you will position yourself for the Edenic command of God to Adam: 1) Be Fruitful, 2) Multiply, 3) Subdue, 4) Replenish and 5) Have Dominion. What you are building or must build will advance the

---

[9] https://www.blueletterbible.org/lang/lexicon/lexicon.cfm?Strongs=H780&t=KJV; Outline of Biblical Usage

[10] Jahn's History of The Hebrew Commonwealth; page 624

kingdom of God and empower you to be Adamic in your life's journey. You are God's new trustee of the earth!

BUILDING REVERSES THE CURSE

We have established that Ararat means the curse is reversed. Now let us apply this to our life today. When Noah built the ark or what God commanded it took him to a place called the curse is reversed. At Ararat the curse was reversed, and shortly thereafter, the covenant of God was revealed. You must be keenly aware completing what God requires is not just about being obedient. That is a primary outcome, however, there are deeper dimensions. What you build has the power to remove the curse from your life. What curse? The curse of poverty. The curse of educational abortion. The curse of opportunity lack. There are many things, areas, and facets that can qualify as curses.

When you build, you not only break the curse from yourself, but others who are assigned to you. Noah's obedience reversed the curse from his family. Noah's obedience reversed the curse from a civilization that had not yet been born, but would ultimately be born as the fruit of Noah's obedience and emerge in a land of no curses. Can you imagine yourself as a bible hero? You are called and chosen. You are God's answer in the earth. You must be in place and realize the power of God is yet being experienced and revealed in many ways. What you build will break, remove, and reverse the curse from your life. Moses was commanded to build a bridge to deliver the Hebrew slaves. When Moses built what God said, it reversed the curse of bondage from the Hebrew nation. When David built what God said, it reversed the curse and amalgamated Judah and the Northern Tribes into one nation of wealth, peace, and prosperity.

When Yeshua built what God said, it reversed the curse of sin, death, hell, and the grave. It also shifted the world to the gateway of salvation, eternal life, liberty, justification, glorification, and so much more. When the Apostles built what God said, more than 3,000 souls were saved in one day!

You are reading this book because the Holy Spirit directed your desire and steps to purchase the key to your success. This book is empowering you to build what God has called and chosen you to do! I command you to BUILD in the Name of Yeshua the Messiah. You cannot break if you do not build. Building does not infer or mean easy, however, it does mean, the provisions are available and the resources are set for your success. You must amass what you need and complete what God has said. You are God's modern-day Noah. The "rest" of God cannot be manifest until you build! God has a rest for you and your family. When you build your business, it will create wealth that will allow you to finance the Kingdom of God and your family. Are you not tired of the perpetuation of poverty and lack over your family? Rise up and build and allow God to bless what you build so the curse can be reversed from your family. Many say that they come from a line of individuals who have never graduated from college. Your call is assigned to reverse that curse from your family line and perpetuate a new record of those who have college degrees. You must build!

BIULD WHAT YOU ARE CALLED TO DO

Frustration occurs when we find ourselves doing what we can do versus doing what we are called to do. Because you have been endowed with various abilities and gifts, you can do many things. However, this can lead to frustration and depression. Being busy doing a function is not the same as doing a fulfilling function. Though there are challenges involved with ministry, running a business, being an artist, etc., there is still a sense of fulfillment knowing you are synchronized with your purpose in life and its destiny. Anything outside of what you are called to do creates frustration. This is why there are many people on jobs, in ministry, and in daily routines that keep them from living a fulfilling life. Always remember, **"building puts you in position; *not-building* keeps you in place!"** To explain this let us go to physics and juxtapose kinetic and potential energy.

According to the Laws of Physics, kinetic energy is energy of motion while potential energy is energy of position[11]. Kinetic energy shown in my example (fig. 1), is created when an outside force performs an action that produces movement. Potential energy (fig. 2) is stored because of its position. Consider Figure 1 for a moment. Many of us are moving through life kinetically. When an outside force moves upon us we then exert energy. This perhaps can have its positive purpose, however, it is key to remember that kinetic energy needs an outside occurrence to create movement. This is why many people are trapped in life. Many individuals are creative, however, the job they are on moves upon them with an outside force (called a directive) to create something for the benefit of the company and not themselves. They are then frustrated because they cannot release their energy or power for their purpose and passion. In the church, kinetic operation can become incarcerating, in that, many people in church need outside affirmation for personal production. When people find out they can control your productivity by affirmations and applause—they will. You must learn that operation in life is to be God-motivated rather than self-motivated. Always remember, the people who heralded hosanna at the triumphal entry of

---

[11] Physics Made Simple by Ira M. Freeman, William J. Durden (Revised by); Broadway Books 9780385242288

Yeshua were the same people who cried crucify Him on the way to the cross!

Knowing potential energy is stored, it is not relative to its environment or outside forces.   More importantly you must see the correlation of you to shifting to potential rather than kinetic operation. Noah had the power to build the ark stored in him by God before he was born. Moses had deliverer stored up in him before he came to Pharaoh's courts. Yeshua had salvation stored up in Him before He went to Calvary.   And YOU have power stored up in you to fulfill God's dream and purpose for your life. Building puts you in place to release the potential of God that has been stored in you When you do not build, you are merely living life kinetically being shifted or moved by another's desire, whim, or plot. Some of you are reading this book and you have been laid off from work. You were laid off because someone made a kinetic decision that shifted you to the unemployment line. Take off your garment of pity and mourning and shift your life to a dimension where God determines your work schedule and not another individual. Does this mean that everyone is a business owner and no one belongs in corporate America? Not at all. If you are called to operate in corporate America, be a shifter, a shaker, and a maker.   Arise and run the division rather than working on the line. Be a decision maker. Become the director of nursing rather than just a staff nurse.   The more we place ourselves in position as Kingdom citizens, the more we will influence our outcome and the outcome of others to the desired will of God which is abundant life (John 10:10).

When you learn to live life doing what you are called to do verses what you can do, you will eliminate dimensions of frustration and depression. I learned about a gift graph from one of the many seminars I attend. When you look at the graph, the horizontal line is the x-axis or what you are called to do. The vertical line is the y-axis or what you can do. If your 'y coordinate' or 'what you can do' number is higher than your 'x coordinate' or 'what you are called to do' number, you will find yourself in frustration and often depression because of the lack of self-fulfillment. (See fig. 3) Any percentage left unshaded is called frustration or the mismanagement of potential. You want to move your numbers from doing what you can do to doing what you are called to do. This will bring you peace, contentment, and happiness.

You MUST build who you are and what God has said to you. The Kingdom is depending upon you. There are things in the world that will not change until you are in place. Moses built himself as the deliverer God had chosen him to be and was responsible for the release of over one million Hebrews who were in Egyptian bondage. David built himself as a king as God had chosen and established peace in Israel and garnered massive wealth for the nation. Samuel build himself as a prophet of God and the bible says, "So the Philistines were subdued and they did not come anymore within the border of Israel. And the hand of the Lord was against the Philistines all the days of Samuel (1 Samuel 7:13)." Remarkable! One man in place positioned the nation to be free from their enemy. You are that one man in place! You are that individual who must build. Build yourself into a position that allows you to free your family and change the generational dysfunction and curse into a perpetual blessing and bountifulness. Build yourself into the desire of God and change the trajectory of your church or congregation. The absence of your gifting creates a breach in the fortification of the kingdom. When a person does not rise to maturity, the commission of God is not merely fulfilled by another individual. Please rehearse the fact that no matter what Peter's failure was, Yeshua only established a particular operation of apostolic authority in him. In Peter was apostolic authority. Without Peter, there would have been an apostolic void. You must build who you are at the command of God. YOU are the answer to a spiritual need or kingdom strategy in the earth. Every time there was a deficiency in the earth, God sent a man as the answer. You are the Joshua who defeats Amalek. You are the Paul sent to minister to the new testament churches. These are the days of Noah in instant replay and you are set God in time to be in The Kingdom for such a time as this.

No matter where you are in life right now, no matter what age, no matter what the economic or social status, receive afresh the words of Philippians 3:13, "Brethren, I do not regard myself as having laid hold of it yet; but one thing I do: forgetting what lies behind and reaching forward to what lies ahead, I press on toward the goal for the prize of the upward call of God in Christ Jesus." God wants you to forget about past failures, missed opportunities, and mismanaged resources and start again! The sooner you build, the faster the curse will be reversed!

The Rhythm of The Wind

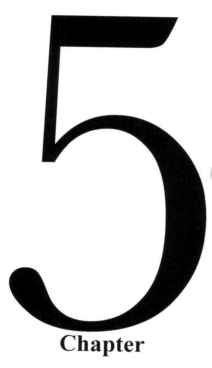

Chapter

"When God breaks the curse, you must walk where The Spirit has been blowing."

Once the curse of the flood was ended, the bible tells us the next event that occurred. Genesis 8:1 reads, "But God remembered Noah and all the beasts and all the cattle that were with him in the ark; and God caused a wind to pass over the earth, and the water subsided." This passage speaks volumes to me in how we should conduct ourselves after a curse has been reversed. Note the scripture declares God caused a wind to pass over the earth. The wind prepared the place where Noah was called! It also prepared the earth for Noah to disembark the ark and step out into his tomorrow. Again, we know wind is a type of the Spirit. Dimensionally we can see God sent His Spirit into the earth to prepare it for Noah's arrival. In like manner, after the curse has been reversed for you, you must know that God has already sent His Spirit to prepare the place of your arrival. This brings to mind Psalm 37:23, "The steps of a man are established by the Lord, And He delights in his way." Your post-curse steps have been ordered by God. Victory and success shall be your portion.

God has a record of sending a wind before a victory! In the account of the exodus of Israel from Egypt, Israel finds themselves trapped (or so they thought) by the Egyptian Army in the rear, mountains to their side and a sea in front of them. Let us rehearse how God delivered them by reviewing Exodus 14:21, "Then Moses stretched out his hand over the sea; and the LORD swept the sea back by a strong east wind all night and turned the sea into dry land, so the waters were divided." As God reversed the curse of Egyptian bondage, He delivered Israel by sending them through the Red Sea—on dry ground! How was this possible? God sent a strong east wind to change the challenge into deliverance! Though the natural appearance was an east wind blowing, spiritually speaking, it was symbolic of the Spirit of God blowing and altering the physical state of the challenge and changing it into a crossover. Instead of Israel trying to cross over on mud and silt, they were able to crossover on dry ground. How? Because God sent them to walk where The Spirit had already been blowing.

Even God operated by the same law in creation. Genesis 1:2 states, "The earth was formless and void, and darkness was over the surface of the deep, and the Spirit of God was moving over the surface of the waters." Before He spoke "let there be light", "let there be a firmament", or "let dry land appear", He sent The Spirit to hover over chaos changing it from chaos to a performance platform. This is exactly what God did for Noah. Before Noah stepped out of the ark, the wind or the Spirit had already been blowing to prepare the place Noah would inhabit and fulfill his mission in life. In like manner this chapter is to make you aware that for every day of your life, as well as, every phase of ministry, God sends his Spirit before you to prepare your environment, world or platform before you get there. We will discuss this further in a moment.

WHAT IS SPIRIT?

In my study of Hebrew at the university I am learning that eastern thinking, which includes Hebrew thinking, is not based on abstract thought. Hebrew thought is concrete and deals with function, not appearance. In other words, if a professor showed a pencil to a western thinker, western thought would influence defining the pencil by its appearance—"it is yellow with an red eraser and black led." If the professor showed the same pencil to an eastern thinker, eastern thought would influence defining the pencil by its function—"it is an instrument used to make my thoughts visible." How you think determines how you will comprehend spirit. If we attempt to define spirit by western abstract thinking it will be difficult because spirit and the spirit realm is invisible to the natural eye. So how would we describe what we cannot see? If we define spirit by eastern thinking and most particularly for this book, Hebrew thinking, we can define spirit by describing its function. Rabbi Moen, the dean of the university I attend defines spirit as "the summary of God's handiwork. Spirit is God—active in hidden ways that are occasionally viewed by man." With these definitions, we understand that spirit is not abstract, it is a force, a realm, and a world. When Noah disembarked the ark, God had already sent the Holy Spirit to prepare the way for Noah. The Spirit has already released "the summary of God's handiwork" that was assigned to bless and propel Noah's purpose! Glory to God! How liberating it will be if you and I can comprehend everyday we rise up, every time we move forward on an idea God has given us, every opportunity we advance to avail ourselves to be used by Him, He precedes us by sending out His Spirit to release the summary of God's handiwork that is assigned to us. WE CANNOT FAIL!

This should help us comprehend how David slew Goliath. God sent His Spirit into the battle ahead of David to release the summary of His handiwork which was the destruction of Goliath. How did Joshua bring down the walls of Jericho? God sent His Spirit to the walls ahead of Joshua and the nation of Israel to release the summary of His handiwork which was the destruction of the wall, entrance into the city, and victory for His children. As I am writing this book, I prophesy—"God is going to release the summary of His handiwork into your life. You are going to begin to reap a backlog of opportunities, blessings, and activations that are yours! Now! In the Name of Yeshua the Mighty God." There are somethings that you have been fighting, working, and believing for that you are going to begin to see come into your life and destiny. They were not delayed by sin or failure, but rather until they were revealed to you they are finished in the Spirit realm. The prophetic power of God that is backing the writing of this book is releasing those things to you now. You are not only reading a good book, you are receiving and releasing the summary of God's handiwork for this dimension of your life. Stop for a moment and give God a praise for what He just released to you then ask Him to give you precision to perceive those things which have just been activated in your world!

THE RHYTHM OF DELIVERANCE

In comprehending how God operates, we must now consider another valuable principle concerning the operation of The Spirit of God in your life. To make this concept clear, we'll begin by paralleling several dimensions of revelation. First, let us consider the law of God hidden in plain sight in Genesis 1:26-27, 31. It reads, "26 Then God said, 'Let Us make man in Our image, according to Our likeness; and let them rule over the fish of the sea and over the birds of the sky and over the cattle and over all the earth, and over every creeping thing that creeps on the earth.' 27 God created man in His own image, in the image of God He created him; male and female He created them. 31 God saw all that He had made, and behold, it was very good. And there was evening and there was morning, the sixth day." Here we first establish that God created man on the sixth day.

Now let us review Genesis 2:1-3, "1 Thus the heavens and the earth were completed, and all their hosts. 2 By the seventh day God completed His work which He had done, and He rested on the seventh day from all His work which He had done. 3 Then God blessed the seventh day and sanctified it, because in it He rested from all His work which God had created and made." When we juxtapose both passages, it reveals a powerful reality.

God's seventh day was Adam's first day because God's design is that man enters into destiny on the "rest" of God where all things are completed and accomplished. When God sends his rest it is so that The Kingdom can BUILD. Let's consider further examples.

How did Adam receive His impartations from God? The answer is couched in the passage that exposes Adam's failure. Today, we look beyond Adam's failure to illuminate this valuable principle. Genesis 3:8a states, "They heard the sound of the Lord God walking in the garden in the cool of the day..." What many bibles define as the cool of the day is the Hebrew word RUACH[12] which means wind, breath, mind and spirit. God came to Adam in the ruach of the day and that is where He imparted unto Adam his mind. With this impartation, Adam is able to cultivate the Garden, subdue the earth, and dominate it. The ruach of God prepared him for the task. Adam can now build because he has been set in the ruach or rest of God. This is God's law and rhythm, which is defined as movement or procedure with uniform or patterned recurrence of a beat, accent, or the like[13].

In the purpose of Noah, Noah (whose name means rest) was used by God as the dimension upon which the earth would be reestablished. God had to establish rest as the platform to build and Noah was that rest. That's why Genesis 5:29 says, "Now he called his name Noah, saying, "This one will give us rest from our work and from the toil of our hands *arising* from the ground which the Lord has cursed." Noah was called to establish

---

[12] https://www.blueletterbible.org/lang/lexicon/lexicon.cfm?Strongs=H7307&t=KJV

[13] http://www.dictionary.com/browse/rhythm

rest after The Flood so the earth could be reestablished and rebuilt.

Walk In The Rhythm of The Wind

Now that we see how God established the rhythm of the wind in the Old Testament let us look to see the New Testament. The Gospel of Matthew 27:50 records, "And Jesus cried out again with a loud voice, and yielded up His spirit [ruach]." Remember once the rest of God is established, it creates a platform to build. Let's look forward in The Gospel of Matthew 27:51 to see what is about to happen. It tells us, "And behold, the veil of the temple was torn in two from top to bottom..." When the veil of the temple was torn in two it represented the old establishment of the tabernacle and temple was complete and now there would be the establishment or the building of a new temple. When Yeshua exhaled the Spirit of God in him it created the ruach—the wind or the rest upon which God would build. The repetition or the rhythm was established and God kept and keeps consistent with His laws.

God wants you to walk in the rhythm every day of your life. Remember how God walked with Adam in the cool or in the ruach of the day? This is teaching us that God has ordered a ruach for everyday of your life! The ruach is provided by God, but the relationship to receive it is provided by you! This is why Jude 20 says, "But you, beloved, building yourselves up on your most holy faith, praying in the Holy Spirit." When you pray in the Holy Ghost you are releasing the ruach (wind, spirit) into the atmosphere. We established earlier, once the ruach or rest of God is present, building can take place.

Take the powerful, vital, and practical chapter and apply it immediately to your life. I promise you will begin to see an immediate change in your environment and lifestyle. The bible shares in Psalm 37:23 "The steps of a man are established by the Lord, And He delights in his way." God has ordered a ruach for your today...did you walk in it?

Build To Excel

"Do not plant that which makes you euphoric; build that which causes you to excel."

Chapter

We now shift into the story of Noah where he and his family have arrived to the new land. The waters have receded, the earth has dried, and now Noah must build the new world— The Kingdom, for God's sake. When Noah exited the ark, the bible says he built an altar to the LORD. The account in Genesis 8:20 reads, "Then Noah built an altar to the Lord, and took of every clean animal and of every clean bird and offered burnt offerings on the altar." Here, we see Noah immediately built what would cause him to excel in the new world—an altar. When we consider the Hebrew definition of altar from the word mizbeach, we note the altar is defined as 1) the place of communication, 2) the place of influence, and 3) the place of exchange. Noah knew to accomplish his role in the new world his tool of choice, was God's choice—the altar. As the place of communication, the altar provided a headquarters from which God could impart into Noah and Noah could speak to God. This communication would provide instruction, revelation, strategy, and more. As the place of influence, the altar would be the place of change. Noah could worship, pray, sacrifice, and God would work on his behalf. Lastly, as the place of exchange, the altar was the place where Noah offered something to receive something. He would offer a sacrifice to receive forgiveness. He would make an offering to raise his spiritual rank. Noah built the thing that would empower him to fulfill the commission God gave to him in Genesis 8:17, "… to be fruitful and multiply…" or in Hebrew the word PARAH which means to bear fruit; to grow; or to increase[14], and to, RAVAH which means to be; to expand; to increase; or to become numerous[15].

---

[14] https://www.blueletterbible.org/lang/lexicon/lexicon.cfm?Strongs=H6509&t=KJV

[15] https://www.blueletterbible.org/lang/lexicon/lexicon.cfm?Strongs=H7235&t=KJV

When Noah completed his actives at the altar it caused God to be moved to do three major things for Noah. Let's look at the account in Genesis 8:21-22 which records,

> "21 The Lord smelled the soothing aroma; and the Lord said to Himself, "I will never again curse the ground on account of man, for the intent of man's heart is evil from his youth; and I will never again destroy every living thing, as I have done.
> 22 "While the earth remains, Seedtime and harvest, And cold and heat, And summer and winter, And day and night Shall not cease."

God inhaled or took in the effects of Noah's altar and it moved Him to give Noah three major empowerments. First, God promised Noah he would not again curse the ground because of mankind's actions. Secondly, He would never destroy every living thing in the same manner as the flood. Thirdly, He placed Noah in a cycle of perpetual prosperity called seedtime and harvest.

When you build an altar to God you too are guaranteed the same benefits. Please be mature in the building and maintaining of your altar to God. Building an altar to God speaks of time, location, and method. How much time do you spend in prayer. Prayer time equates to power engaged and prayer time equates to prophetic output. Prayer is the one significant stone that must initiate the building of the foundation of your self-expression in the earth. A quick prayer in the morning and a quick prayer at night will not yield you what you need to take your life and those connected to you to the next level. You MUST build an altar or build a prayer time. This prayer time is the amount of time you spend with God in strategy. You speaking to God, and most importantly, God speaking back to you!

Next, you must build a location. Your location determines your success! Proverbs 8:17 says, "17 I love them that love me; and those that seek me early shall find me." Psalm 119:164 declares, "Seven times a day do I praise thee because of thy righteous judgments." As you can see, **where you place God in your day determines where success is placed in your destiny.** Finding a location for God, prayer, and worship has to do with finding those times of fellowship that build. I recall the first time I presented an oratorio, my budget was in excess of twenty thousand dollars. God blessed me to secure every dollar. Why? —my location. I built a prayer time for God on a daily basis as it related to this need and nine months prior to the first bill that needed to be paid. This meant I had time to build the budget for nine months before I needed it. The location of prayer in my day showed my connection to God, my understanding of how to excel, and my ability to tap into the resources God had already assigned to my purpose. My wife as a strong intercessor, rises daily before Sunday and prays and communes with the Lord. I am a believer in prayer and give a great portion of my day to praying and decreeing the results I desire to see.

Lastly there is method. I refer to this as praying with intentionality. Some prayers are prayers from the soul as it cries out to our Father for our needs and wants. Other prayers are prayers of strategy which may require focus and a process. I admonish you to make a daily prayer journal. For example, you may be starting a business. Refrain from general prayers to God in a by rote format. Make your prayer strategy daily. If you're starting a business, perhaps one prayer is asking for a release of capital to initiate the business. Another prayer may be about favor in networking and relationships. Another for insight on how to utilize marketing strategies to secure your customer base. The list is endless. **Focused prayer births focused results.** Certainly, God knows your heart. However, to cover needed requests or warfare a simple "Lord bless the business" prayer will not grant you what you need.

BUILDING TO EXCEL vs PLANTING FOR EUPHORIA

As we indicated above, Noah built an altar immediately which caused God to set in motion the laws and favor necessary to secure Noah's success. God gave Noah an empowerment called "seedtime and harvest." The building of the altar was a divine strategy. The planting of the vineyard was human ingenuity. Let's take a closer look into Genesis 9, which reads,

> 20 Then Noah began farming and planted a vineyard.
> 21 He drank of the wine and became drunk..."

When Noah built to excel, he flourished. When he planted for euphoria, he failed. As you shift to the place of promise, you must watch what or who persuades you to plant. You must guard the spiritual seeds God has provided you: prayer, worship, time, money, faith, love, and so many others act as seeds that are empowered to produce things in your life. Watch how you plant these seeds. Watch where you plant these seeds. They are set to produce for you the abundant life promised to you. Because of this, the adversary will be after this power to keep you from excelling in this life.

Many people today are found building that which makes them happy or content at the expense of building that which makes them purposeful. You must not make the same mistake.

Your purpose is not your option. Many individuals in the Kingdom lie dormant, disobedient, and unfruitful because they see God's purpose for their life as an option. The gifts and callings of God are without repentance (Romans 11:29). Yours or His! Once God has set your purpose, He does not change His mind. You are that purpose. Equally important is the fact that your productivity and prosperity is tied to your purpose. If your purpose is absent—so is your prosperity! Consider Genesis 3:17-19,

> 17 Then to Adam He said, 'Because you have listened to the voice of your wife, and have eaten from the tree about which I commanded you, saying, 'You shall not eat from it'; Cursed is the ground because of you; In toil you will eat of it All the days of your life.
> 18 "Both thorns and thistles it shall grow for you; And you will eat the plants of the field;
> 19 By the sweat of your face You will eat bread, Till you return to the ground, Because from it you were taken; For you are dust, And to dust you shall return."

When we consider the true interpretation of the text, God is not "punishing" Adam for His disobedience. God is announcing to Adam the "result" of his disobedience. Because the earth was connected to Adam, when Adam fell all that was connected to him fell also. When Adam was in alignment with his purpose, God provided Eden for him. When he shifted from that alignment, his shift revoked his flow of provision. Now Adam had to work for that which was once freely given. You and I must learn from Adam's costly error and build that which causes us to excel.

Ephesians 1:18-19 teaches us another valuable lesson about remaining connected to your purpose or your call. It reads,

> 18 I pray that the eye of your heart may be enlightened, so that you will know what is the hope of His calling, what are the riches of the glory of His inheritance in the saints,
> 19 and what is the surpassing greatness of His power toward us who believe. These are in accordance with the working of the strength of his might.

This text explains that your purpose is connected to an inheritance of riches, power, and might from God. Have you ever noted that when the prodigal son returned to his father's house he was immediately reconnected to authority and wealth? This is because an individual's purpose is connected to power and prosperity. No matter the call, all God-calls are connected to power and wealth. Your life must take on the trek of pursuing your purpose. The more I shift my life to the full alignment of my purpose exclusively, the more I find that power is afforded to me and wealth is released to me. This is why the adversary wants us to merely exist in a fog. This fog will never reveal to us the true reality of our purpose.

NO MORE TREASURE CITIES

An insightful account comes to us from Exodus 1:8-11 which states,

> 8 Now a new king arose over Egypt, who did not know Joseph.

9 He said to his people, "Behold, the people of the sons of Israel are more and mightier than we

10 Come, let us deal wisely with them, or else they will multiply and in the event of war, they will also join themselves to those who hate us, and fight against us and depart from the land."

11 So they appointed taskmasters over them to afflict them with hard labor. And they built for Pharaoh storage cities, Pithom and Raamses."

Joseph (a descendant of Abraham) was placed in a seat of power within Egypt because of his knowledge and understanding. He became second in command in all of Egypt. After Joseph died the Hebrews continued to become powerful and strong. Because of their might and ability, the Egyptians feared a revolt since so many Hebrews lived within the gates of the city. They craftily placed the Hebrews into slavery.

There are two important findings from this text. The first, when Egypt faced destruction because of a severe famine that had come upon the land, who was it that saved the country from desolation?—Joseph! Joseph, who represents the Kingdom of God had the insight, ingenuity, and know how to save Egypt. Egypt with all her leaders, astrologists, and magicians could not save the nation from hunger and despair. The church was the only answer to impending despair. Joseph kept Egypt from feeling the effects of a seven-year drought. After the death of Joseph, the Egyptians feared the Hebrews, and as a result, placed them in captivity. The very first thing Egypt had the Hebrews do while in captivity was build treasure cities. Notice twice now the Hebrews had the power to save Egypt from a famine and then build them treasure cities.

It is time for you to comprehend the power of God in you as The Kingdom. God has given you the ideas, invention, strategies, and plans to benefit the world. You must begin to invest in yourself and the Kingdom of God in you and refuse to build treasure cities for the world that do not benefit the church. You must be ignited by the apostolic authority of Yeshua afforded to you as a believer and BUILD for the sake of The Kingdom. True apostolic individuals (the new testament empowerment, not merely a denomination) comprehend that we are called to invade the world and its systems and sow the culture and message of The Kingdom until all areas, environments, cities, and nations take on the behavior, mentality, obedience, and vision of The Kingdom. In this season, some are called to the pulpit and others (equally as called and anointed) are called to take position in the political arena, until congress starts acting apostolic! Some are to occupy seats on the school board until the school board has an apostolic majority! As a builder, and most importantly, an apostolic builder, you are called to infiltrate every sector of life. You are called to counter the present culture with the message of The Kingdom. A builder you are and building you must do! I prophesy to your spirit man and declare, "You shall arise and build! In the Name of Yeshua—Amen!"

BUILD FROM THE CLOUD DOWN

The final instruction is a call to build from the cloud down. In Genesis 9:13 we read, "13 I set My bow in the cloud, and it shall be for a sign of a covenant between Me and the earth." The sign of the covenant was in "the cloud." The cloud is the place of God's glory. The cloud is the place of God's source. By this text we learn the covenant or the promise of God was in the cloud.

Noah's altar and God's cloud were connected. God did not give Noah the sign of His promise in the cloud until Noah touched God with His altar. When Noah put his altar in place it positioned him to be aligned with God's cloud and His promise. You must do the same. Your altar is the key to your promise. You cannot build without an altar because the altar produces the cloud. As long as Noah built by his altar experience, we read of no calamity or failure. However, as soon as Noah built or in this case planted without the influence of the altar, he switched from building to excel to building that which was euphoric and that led to failure and defeat. God wants you to be successful and build by the cloud which comes from building at the altar.

Another text that further explains this valuable lesson is found in Exodus 20:18-21,

> 18 All the people perceived the thunder and the lightning flashes and the sound of the trumpet and the mountain smoking; and when the people saw it, they trembled and stood at a distance.
> 19 Then they said to Moses, "Speak to us yourself and we will listen; but let not God speak to us, or we will die."
> 20 Moses said to the people, "Do not be afraid; for God has come in order to test you, and in order that the fear of Him may remain with you, so that you may not sin."
> 21 So the people stood at a distance, while Moses approached the thick cloud where God was.

Here, God called the entire nation of Israel to hear His word and command. Israel opted out of going up into God's presence because of fear. While Moses was up in the cloud receiving

God's commands, the people were in a lower dimension and were given over to the thoughts and creativity of the flesh rather than that of the Spirit. The bible says that while Moses was with God, Israel "rose up to play" (Exodus 32:6). When they began to build without the exposure of God's cloud, they built to a temporary euphoric state that ultimately became the place of death and despair. The scripture further explains what they built in Exodus 32:2-4,

> 2 Aaron said to them, "Tear off the gold rings which are in the ears of your wives, your sons, and your daughters, and bring them to me."
> 3 Then all the people tore off the gold rings which were in their ears and brought them to Aaron.
> 4 He took this from their hand, and fashioned it with a graving tool and made it into a molten calf; and they said, "This is your god, O Israel, who brought you up from the land of Egypt."

When Israel did not go up into the cloud with Moses, instead of building forward for promise, they built backwards towards bondage. The golden calf that they built was connected to the Egyptian bull, Apis, which was sacred to the god Ptah and his symbol[16]. Instead of Israel building what would propel them toward their future, they rebuilt that which represented the bondage of their past. What is just as alarming is they used the wealth God provided them to rebuild a god, the system of Egyptians bondage.

---

[16] https://www.myjewishlearning.com/article/the-golden-calf/

IN CONCLUSION

You and I must learn from this lesson and remain steadfast in ministry at the altar which will secure our success. I admonish you to know that you have been chosen to be present in The Kingdom for such a time as this (Esther 4). You are unique to God's purpose in the earth. I pray this book becomes a guiding force that pushes you to pursue your God-given purpose and the engagement of your presence in the world. God is counting on YOU to occupy until He comes. Wherever this book finds you, GO HIGHER. If you are in the valley, run to the mountaintop. If you are already on the mountaintop, fly to the heavens. You must see yourself as a modern Noah. Be one who refrains from just reading about biblical heroes and become God's hero in the earth. Your personal greatness is as powerful as any present day leader or any biblical champion. You have a command on your life to build. Do not fear—BUILD! Do not come to God with excuses—BUILD! The time signature of heaven is calling for the builders to take position—IN PUBLIC.

Now...Kingdom Come...Will Be Done! Come out of hiding and "Build It In Public!"

21 Day ONE Workout

The following pages are filled with tools to help you further-shape, shape, or reshape your future.

Remember, "Every prophecy needs a strategy in order to be fulfilled."

Therefore, you and I must write, strategize and work to receive that which is ours!

Twenty-One Day Decree

- The scripture declares, "Where the word of a king is there is power." Therefore, I speak and expect!

- The favor of God surrounds me as a shield.

- I see myself as God sees me. I am a BUILDER! I have dominion. I am walking in divine favor.

- According to Ezekiel 36, I prophesy to the mountains surrounding Israel and command them to stretch forth their branches and bless The Kingdom of God and to bless the works of my hands.

- I will not walk in lack. I will not walk in poverty. Windows, open unto me! Doors, open unto me! NOW!

- Let the prophetic winds of God blow upon my home, my family, my promises, and my destiny to equip me for building who I am.

- Starting today, I prophesy, "My seed shall remain and not wither away. Seed multiply! Seed multiply! Seed multiply in the Name of Yeshua!"

- I fall out of agreement with every thing, every person, every spirit, and every weakness that hinders me, my purpose, and my future.

- I am called to rule the earth. I am [men: ISH] or [women: ISHA]. I am made in God's image. I am His reflection in the earth.

- My inheritance is released and coming to me swiftly.

- God is my Rock, my Shield, my Anchor, and my Help.

- Today I will walk, live, and move in the liberty of Yeshua.

- I am God's thought revealed in the earth. I am called to this time. The Kingdom of God needs me. I will NOT fail!

- My borders are shifting my enemies far from me. No weapon formed against me will ever prosper.

- According to Zephaniah 3:10, "The Lord shall rejoice over me with singing."

- Kingdom Come! Favor Come! Power Come! Blessings Come! Expansion Come! Boldness Come! Holy Spirit Come! Holy Spirit Come! Holy Spirit Come!

Vision

In the next 365 days I commit my purpose, time, energy and finances to build (name 1-3 projects):

PROJECT ONE: _____

Start Date: _____ Completion Date: _____

PROJECT TWO: _____

Start Date: _____ Completion Date: _____

PROJECT THREE: _____

Start Date: _____ Completion Date: _____

Network

A vision requires a network. A network is a group of individuals who will give guidance, assistance, or work ethic to what you build.

3 People I need from my present circle:

_____

_____

_____

3 People I need from without my circle or persons I must meet or contact:

_____

_____

_____

Assign a deadline *and stick to it*!

I will contact these individuals by: _____

I completed this task on: _____

Assessment

Name 3 of your strengths (spiritual or natural). Name 5 of your character challenges.

_____

_____

_____

_____

_____

_____

_____

How will you strengthen your challenges?

_____

_____

Plan 1

Every vision requires a well-thought plan. Write your plan below with objectives, goals, and needs. Then follow it through!

_____

_____

_____

_____

_____

_____

_____

_____

_____

_____

_____

_____

Plan 2

Every vision requires a well-thought plan. Write your plan below with objectives, goals, and needs. Then follow it through!

_____

_____

_____

_____

_____

_____

_____

_____

_____

_____

_____

_____

Plan 3

Every vision requires a well-thought plan. Write your plan below with objectives, goals, and needs. Then follow it through!

_____

_____

_____

_____

_____

_____

_____

_____

_____

_____

_____

_____

_____

Quotable

Operate your life and building by these concise but powerful quotes. Live by them and you will also prosper by them.

- "Incomplete assignments today create adversity tomorrow!"

- "If you only fit the opinion of others, you will soon become a misfit to the opinion of God."

- "Life cannot be discovered; it must be revealed."

- "Time is a seed in the hand of a sower.—Sow well!"

- "Stop inviting your enemies to the table because 'you' perceive you need them."

- "No self-pity. There are always more who are for you than there are against you!"

- "You are greater than your zip code. Break limitations!"

- For people who bring up negativity from your past trying to trap you when you know you're forgiven, tell them: "**God forgot about it...only Satan remembers it....who's controlling you?**"

- There is no external voice that can diminish the voice of God for your life!

Let's Build!

I would be honored to have the opportunity to share the revelation and apostolic demonstration God has given me with your congregation or ministry!

For ministry opportunities or seminars, please reach me by emailing: 614kingdomvoice@gmail.com.

- Speaking

- Seminars

- Discussions

- Radio Interviews

Another book packed with power, insight and revelation:

Order
your copy
today!

Available on
Amazon

**"God does not see your challenge...
He sees His CHOICE!"**

This book is designed to take you on a journey to reevaluate your life and the empowerments God has given to you that guarantee your victory!

Change your perception...change your outcome!

Do it today by ordering "Look Again: Matters of Perception". This addition to your library will produce!

Made in the USA
Monee, IL
15 September 2021